another 500 Heartwarming Expressions

For Crafting, Painting, Stitching and Scrapbooking

by Sandy Redburn
Artwork by Suzanne Carillo and Shelly Ehbrecht

Crafty Secrets Publications
15430 78A Ave.
Surrey, B.C. Canada
V3S 8R4

ISBN 0-9686648-0-6   Printed in Canada

Table of Contents · Book 3

Themes for Border & Expression Pages

• •

There is a smorgasbord of creative supplies and helpful aids for lettering expressions onto an almost endless array of surfaces. Check with your local retail stores for products from the manufacturers listed below.

Zig Pens, Markers &
Lettering Books
EK Success
(Zig Markers)
611 Industrial Rd.
Carlstadt, NJ 07072-6507
Phone (201) 939-5404
Fax   (201) 939-4511

Pigma Ink Pens &
Specialty Markers
Sakura of America
(Pigma® Ink Products)
30780 San Clemente St.
Hayward, CA 94544-7131
Phone (510) 475-8880
Fax   (510) 475-0973

Needle Craft
Alphabets
ASN Publishing
1455 Linda Vista Drive
San Marcos, CA 92069
Phone (760) 471-2320
Fax   (760) 591-0230

Oil Pencils, Woodburning
Tools, Blank Wood Pieces
Walnut Hollow Farm. Inc.
1409 State Road 23
Dodgeville, WI
53533-2112
Phone (608) 935-2341
Fax   (608) 935-3029

Introduction

Here we are back with our new revised Book #3, from the Heartwarming Expressions series. Previously titled Another 425 Heartwarmin' Expressions, this book now includes over 500 Heartwarming Expressions along with 40 brand new border pages!

As many of us look for more simple pleasures in our complex, often stressful world, we have begun to focus more on our families, friendships, spirituality, values, homes and health. Adding some heartwarming and humorous expressions to our gifts, greeting cards, scrapbooks, seasonal and home decor craft projects, is an easy and fun way to create more warm fuzzies and smiles.

As you flip through this book please give some thought to all those people you regularly buy gifts for. There is an expression to suit almost any occasion or theme. Giving a handcrafted gift truly shows personal time and thought has been given to the receiver. Best of all, your gift can grace someone's life with a hug from your heart.

We hope this third collection of expressions will leave your imagination and creative spirit brimming with inspirational ideas.

Thanks Are Due

There are many people involved in the creation of a book and they deserve a round of applause and a big thank you! To all the creative souls who passed on their favorite expressions, including Brenda Rintisch, Lynn Ujvary, Julie Weibe and Margo Helliwag. To Bev Sundeen for her contributions to the artwork. To Diane at Splash Graphics, Claire Patterson at Webcom, Peter Fiddler, and my mom Rachel Van Tassell for their hard work. Thanks to my family for their ongoing patience and support, while I spent many months in our dining room in an "endless paste-up party", fitting all the expressions and artwork onto each page. I love doing some of the lettering but I saved all the fancy lettering for Suzanne and Shelly. So, the biggest thank you must go to them, because their talented hard work has added special personality to every page in this book.

Finally a big heartwarming thanks to you for your support and response to these books. Have fun spreading smiles!

Sandy

Sandy Redburn's dedication to inspiring others' creativity includes writing, publishing and teaching seminars since 1993. As the author of the Heartwarming Expressions Books, Sandy admits to being addicted to creating new expressions but promises to stop now at 500 (actually this book has over 500). She owns three rhyming dictionaries and also loves to use great quotes from Miss Piggy to Shakespeare. She runs her successful home-based business with the help of her husband and three daughters.

Shelly Ehbrecht's speciality is in her wonderful lettering and she has contributed greatly to this book from its birth, helping to make it all possible. Shelly has received her CPD, (Certified Professional Demonstrators Diploma) and enjoys teaching folk art painting classes. She is also a full time registered nurse on a maternity ward and lives a happy and busy life with her husband and two daughters.

Suzanne Carillo is a multi-talented artist who was brought on board in 1999 to help with the illustrations and artistic lettering in this book. Now in this revised edition Suzanne's whimsical and humorous artwork and hand lettering grace so many pages, her name has been added to the cover. Suzanne works as a freelance artist.

Easy Lettering Tips & Tricks

Lettering is not as hard as you may think and, as you will see throughout this book, by no means does it have to be perfect or for that matter straight! You can do your lettering by free hand, or you can trace our expressions and designs right onto your project.

If you would like your lettering larger, you can recreate any expression using the enlarged alphabets in the back of this book. You may also photocopy any expressions and have them enlarged or reduced to fit your personal needs.

Trace or pencil on your lettering first, to get your spacing right. A good eraser and see-through plastic ruler are two very helpful tools for lettering.

It's Easy!

1. Use a pencil & ruler. Lettering does not have to be even - just consistent.
2. Hold pens in an upright position.
3. When possible pull your pen rather than push.
4. Add extra embellishments to create different styles.
5. Get bravely creative - but remember practice and patience.

Dot lettering is one of the easiest styles of printing to reproduce. Remember you do not have to embellish your letters with dots. As you will see, you can change your printing style by adding hearts, stars, flowers, snowflakes, holly, stitching lines and more!

There are countless design books available, with wonderful patterns you can incorporate with our expressions. Look around you for inspiration and be sure to read our list of *99 Places To Put An Expression* inside the front cover. Once you start, you will find life offers endless "perfect spots" to add a Heartwarming Expression or tickle some funny bones.

 Magic   Holly-days   Kisses.   country

Worms   raining   Whistle   Superstar

Macho   Cool   stressed   School   Heart

Using Pens & Markers

Using Pens and markers is easy and fun because they are now available in a multitude of tip styles, sizes and colors in both water based and permanent inks. Water based pens work well for a variety of paper crafts, but permanent pigma ink markers won't fade and can be used on a large variety of surfaces. The manufacturers of these markers all agree you should hold your pens in an upright position so the tip has full contact with the writing surface. It may feel a bit awkward but will give you the true essence of the pen tip.

You will also find you have better control of your pen when you pull it towards you rather than pushing it away.

Our samples below show how different combinations of pen tips can give your lettering lots of personality and style. They were done with black ink, so imagine adding colour. There are several helpful lettering books available, as well as computer software with fonts that look hand lettered.

Quiltin'

Letters - Pigma Micron 05
Embellishments - Pigma Micron 01

Have a Bloomin Good Day

Letters - Pigma Micron 03

Don't get yer knickers in a knot!

Letters - Zig 08 Millennium
Embellishments - Pigma Micron 01

DISCOVER WILDLIFE - Have Kids

Letters - Pigma Micron 01

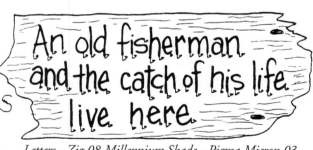

An old fisherman and the catch of his life live here.

Letters - Zig 08 Millennium, Shade - Pigma Micron 03

There's snowman I'd rather be with

Letters - Pigma Micron 03, Embellishments - Zig 01 Millennium

Miracles grow where you plant them

Sakura Dual-point Identi Pen: Letters - the fine point   Embellishments - the extra fine point

Creative Possibilities

Photo copying

Our Designs & Border Pages

You can use the expressions and designs in this book as clip art to create album pages, cards, tags, magnets stationary and more. *You don't have to cut the pages of this book.* Please read our copyright restrictions on the first page of this book. For your personal use, have the designs you want to use enlarged or reduced on a good quality photocopier. From your copy, cut out the expression, graphics, border etc. and lay them out on a piece of paper. Attach them with a glue stick, removeable tape or rubber cement. Copy this page onto your final "good" paper or card stock, which you can decorate with colored pens or pencils. You can also have color copies made of your work. Color copies are perfect for scrapbooks, calenders and decoupaging onto projects. Many people prefer to use a light box and simply trace the design they want to use. Anything you want to save for years should be copied or traced onto acid free paper.

Transferring Tips

Depending on your project, you may want to transfer expressions and designs from this book. Once you decide on what you want to use, lay tracing paper over it and draw it out. Lay your traced design on your project surface and slip some transfer paper in between your design and prepared surface. Trace the outline with a stylus or empty pen tip. Saral®

manufactures a wax free transfer paper that works on wood, fabric, metal, glass, tile, ceramic, etc. Wax free paper will not clog the tips of your markers and pens. Heat activated transfer pencils also work well on fabric.

Expressions For Scrap booking & Paper Crafts

You can use our expressions to create your own special occasion and seasonal decorations, birthday cards, scrapbooks, framed calligraphy, greeting cards, gift tags, invitations, stationary and wrapping paper. Jazz up your projects with colored pencils and inks, watercolors, metallic markers, glitter pens, decorative punches and scissors, templates, stencils, stickers, rubber stamps, 3D or traditional decoupage, paper castings, ribbon and more! Again if you are creating anything you wish to preserve for many years use acid free supplies.

Expressions On Wood

If you don't have a steady hand for doing your lettering with a paintbrush, don't worry, you can cheat and use permanent markers. When you apply dots to letters on wood, use paint rather than your pen tip. Not only will you save the life of your pens, you can create dots faster and more consistent in size using paint. Dots can be made using a brush tip, stylus or embossing tool. We use corsage pins and various plastic headed pins for different size dots. Stick the pins into the eraser tip of a pencil and just dip the head into paint. When using permanent markers for lettering, test any varnish first. Krylon manufactures a Clear Matte Spray Finish, which won't make the ink in permanent markers bleed.

Expressions On Fabric

Pre-wash fabric to remove any sizing and don't use fabric softener. You can use a heat activated transfer pencil, or place some fabric transfer paper between your design and fabric (following all manufacturers' directions). Before painting your transferred design, place a piece of cardboard under your fabric surface (a cookie sheet will also work). Use fabric paints or regular acrylics mixed with a textile medium. Look for quality brushes recommended for textile painting, fabric markers, or use the mini tips on paint bottles to do lettering. You can also have a copy centre put your design onto transfer paper, which you can iron onto clothing, quilts, pillows and more. Remember any lettering must be mirrored or it will transfer backwards.

Expressions On Glass & Ceramics

Paint expressions on an assortment of dishware, tiles, glasses, vases and decor. You can use traditional ceramic techniques and glazes, or cheat and use the new glass and ceramic paints. We love the new paint liner pens which are great for lettering. These paints should be baked in an oven for a permanent finish.

Expressions By Needle & Thread

Stitching includes an array of techniques for applying expressions, using fancy threads, floss, yarns, ribbons or beads. Machine or hand embroidery, hand stitching on felt, needlepoint, cross stitch, plastic canvas, quilted appliqués and silk ribbon embroidery are all popular decorative embellishments. You can stitch expressions on everything baby bibs to bumper pads, decorative pillows, wall samplers, aprons, linens, sweatshirts, vests, jumpers, jean jackets, boxer shorts, ties, bathrobes and more!

The American School of Needlework (ASN Publishing) is a great source for cross stitch design books. They have generously donated the cross stitch alphabets on page 87 in this book. If you don't want to stitch by hand, check out the amazing things you can create with an embroidery machine today!

Embellishing Your Expressions

Depending on the materials and style of your project you can also embellish expressions with raffia, jute, wire, paper twist, ribbons, lace, trims, buttons, charms, shells, fabric motifs, lace appliqués or miniature accessories. To add extra personality to a collection of dolls or stuffed animals, try creating some mini signs to add to the display. You are only limited by your imagination, so go on . . . get creative!

When angels sing ... flowers bloom

Angels help radiate his love from above

Fairy Duties
☆ Watch Over Children
☆ Sprinkle Sleepy Dust
☆ Collect Lost Teeth
☆ Listen to Hopes & Dreams

My Gardian Angel watches over me and keeps me safe as safe can be

When the first baby laughed, for the first time,
his laugh broke into a million pieces,
and they all went skipping about.
That was the beginning of fairies.
— J.M. Barrie

Wish I May,
Wish I Might
See a Wee Pixie
Tonight

Good Night Sweet Prince (Princess)
and flights of angels sing thee to thy rest.
— Shakespeare

Secret Garden
Fairies Gather Here

If we all acted more angelic, the world would feel more heavenly

DON'T WAIT
until you get to heaven
to act like an ANGEL

Guardian Angels
from up above
Please watch over
those we love

Angels bring comfort from up above,
on wings of faith and whispers of love

Have a fairy enchanting time

Angels are messengers from above,
sent to spread God's light and love.

A wing and a prayer
can take you anywhere

Sweet enough
to be an angel

Angel

God watches over us
with tender loving care
and when we need a helping hand
an angel's always there

A fairy nice person
&
an old troll
live here

Be an angel,
God loves a helping hand

There Is A Special Blessing In My Life: YOU

Blessings

Lord Let Your Love and Grace
Shine Upon and Bless this Place

Count Your Blessings Every Day & See Them Grow In Every Way

Bless Today in Every Way

May the road rise up to meet you
May the wind be at your back.
— Irish Blessing

Choose Joy!

God loves us
Pass it along

May all the world be richly blessed
With lasting peace and happiness

Were there no God,
we would all be in this glorious world
with grateful hearts and no one to thank
— Christina Rossetti

For today
and its blessings,
I owe the world
an attitude of gratitude

Count your blessings
not your cash

Life!

Each day is a gift to unfold
Cherish each one, because the present has no mold

Merry Merry Holly-days

Christmas Blessings
wrapped in warm wishes
tied with joy &
sent with love

Peace on Earth
& Goodwill to All

Wise men still adore him

Berry Kissmas

Wishing you JOY
be-Claus it's Christmas

CHRISTMAS IS SNOW MUCH FUN

Priority Post
North Pole or Bust!

SANTA EXPRESS

Wishing you a Christmas brimming
with love, laughter and joyful memories

Season's Tweetings

Be good for goodness sake

Santa's Workshop
Elves' Entrance

The Perfect Man
He's quiet and sweet
and if he gives you any grief
you can bite his head off

15

There's snowman I'd rather be with... CHRISTMAS

There's Snowplace Like Home For The Holidays

Yo Snow

Cold nose... warm heart.

Shaped from warm hands and young ♥s

There is snow-girl like my girl Frosty

Be warm Inside & Out

Chill out! I'm a really cool guy just a little bit flakey

WANTED
Summer house to rent
Freezer space preferred

The Christmas present most often returned
LOVE

To my Family:
Yule always be the best part of Christmas
xox

May the spirit of Christmas fill you with love and peace, spreading goodwill that will never cease.

Deck the malls ... with all my money.

Who Needs Santa?
- I Have VISA

Like a Snowflake You're one of A Kind

Welcome to the Ranch

Howdy Ya'll

Country

Don't look back, the posse's gaining

Happiness is....

HOME ON THE RANGE

Being a True Cowgirl

Please tell my Mom: Cowboys don't take baths, We just dust off

Speak, your mind.... But ride a fast horse.

We had an Udderly Moovelous Time

Good Moo's from the Herd We've added one udder.

BABY CALF

Servin up the best darn vittles this side of Texas

No Villains or Varmints Allowed

You're the apple of my eye, You're the cream of the crop, You're the ice cream on my pie and the cherry on top!

Don't get yer knickers in a knot!

19

Doggone Good to T-bone

Our dog may be no perfect pedigree,
just the perfect mixture we agree...
A mutt!

Will work 4 bones

My dog is my best friend

HOME IS WHERE YOUR DOG IS

Tweet Dreams

Rent for a Song

Fly by night

Fly Right Inn

My dog doesn't care
if I'm rich, witty or slim,
I'll always be a best friend
to him.

Doggie Bag

FOR WRENT Cheap, cheap

Birdie Retweet

We're only staying together
for the sake of the dog.

Just say No
to chicken nuggets

Beastly Weather Today

When it's raining cats and dogs,
Don't step in the poodles.

DON'T LOOK
Birdies Bathing

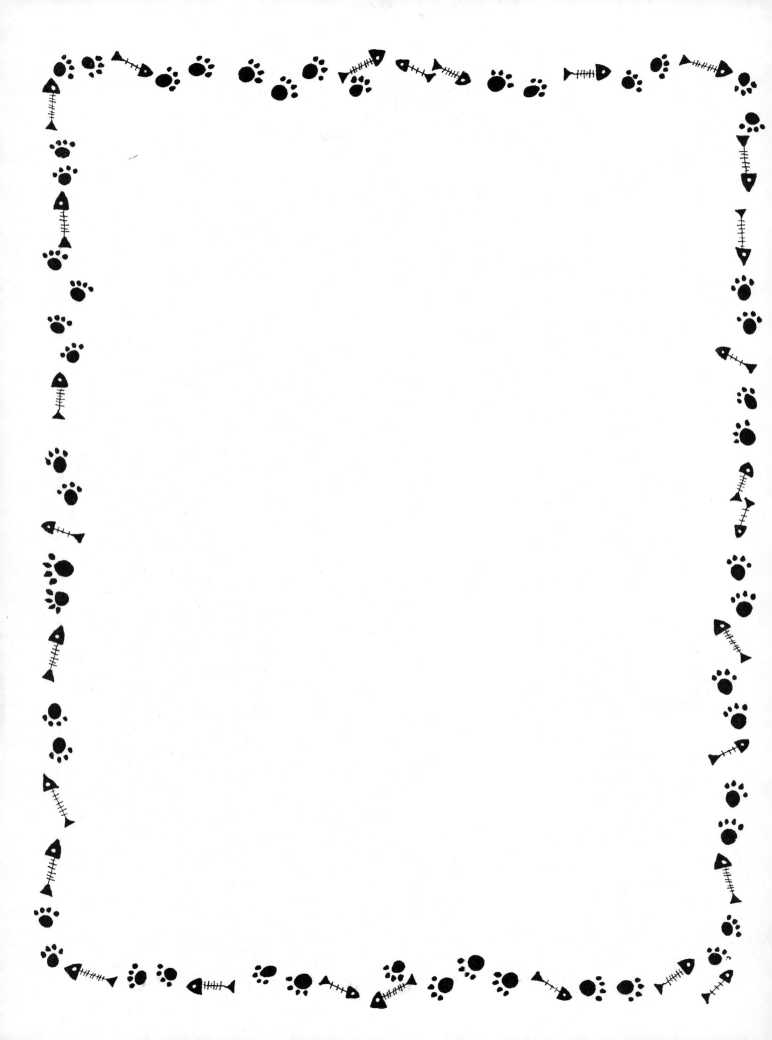

What's Mew?

Home is where the meow is

Critters

Welcome to the Cat House

In this house, the cat is in charge

Tiger in training

How wonderful to do nothing & rest afterwards

Every life should have 9 cats!

I ♥ Birdies

My kitty makes everyday PURR-FECT

I'm not rude. I've got cat-i-tude!

Cats understand the importance of naps.

smarty cat

FURRY TAILS MY FUR LADY

Pussed off!

Purr-ority Post

Fur-class

Just for Mew

Feline purr-fect tuna-night

The heart frames can hold photos or names. You can reduce or enlarge the frames to add more or fewer frames for family members. You might also include pets.

Our ♥ Family ♥ is ♥ a ♥ Work ♥ of ♥ Heart

FAMILY

We may not all be from the same family tree But we make a great team Don't you agree?

One Classy Lady My Mom

Grandpas are like libraries Full of good stories

When you teach your son you teach your son's son
— The Talmud

Family Reunions are Fabulous Fun

You're an ALL STAR
Son in our Hall of Fame

No picture gallery is richer in the happy images of children than a grandmother's heart
— Helen Frank

MOM
Thanks for hatching me

Daddy, You are my favorite guy to hold hands with

I've been blessed twice, to call you my sister (brother mother father) and a dear friend

Daughters don't come any sweeter than You

27

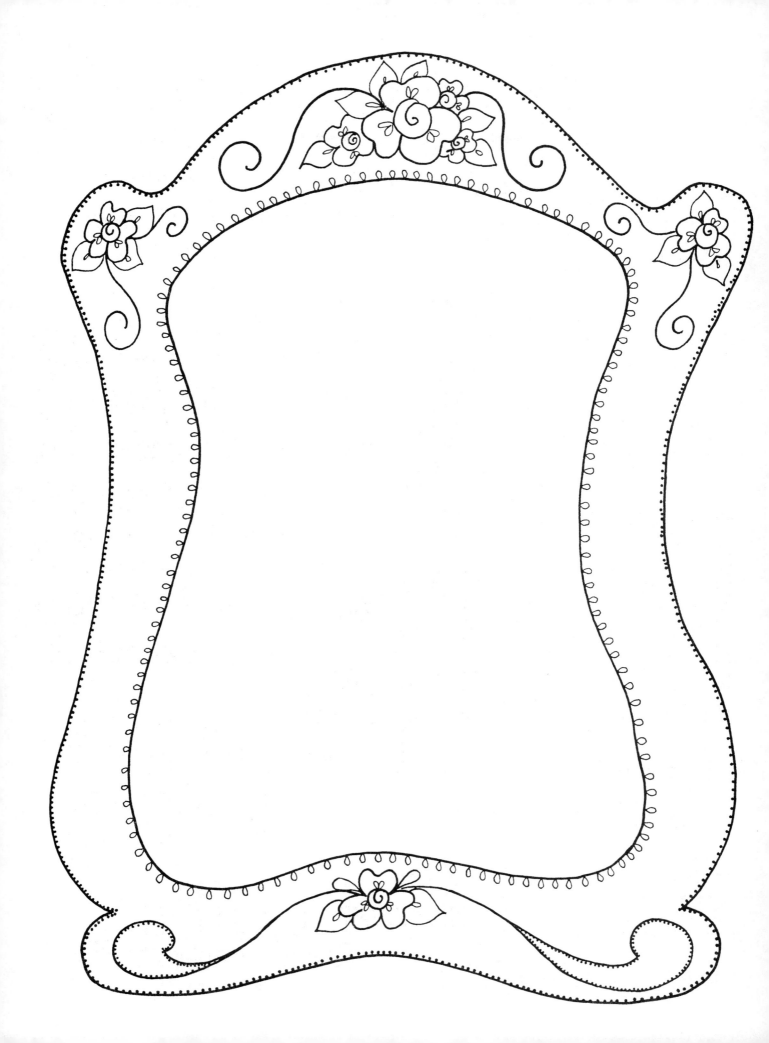

Family is another name for love

FAMILY

My Mom is.
- My Guardian Angel
- My Heart Mender
- My Best Friend

Love & Trust
The Foundation of a Family

Dad,
no matter
how tall I grow
I will always
look up to you

Mother mender of Hearts

Mothers receive the highest pay PURE LOVE

Great Dads get promoted to Grand·dads

I may not be rich but I have some priceless jewels... my grandchildren

You put the GRAND in Grandmother

Best Gramps I ever saw.

GRANDPARENTS are Gods gift to Children

It's hard to be humble when you're a Grandmother

CAUTION: Grandparents at Play

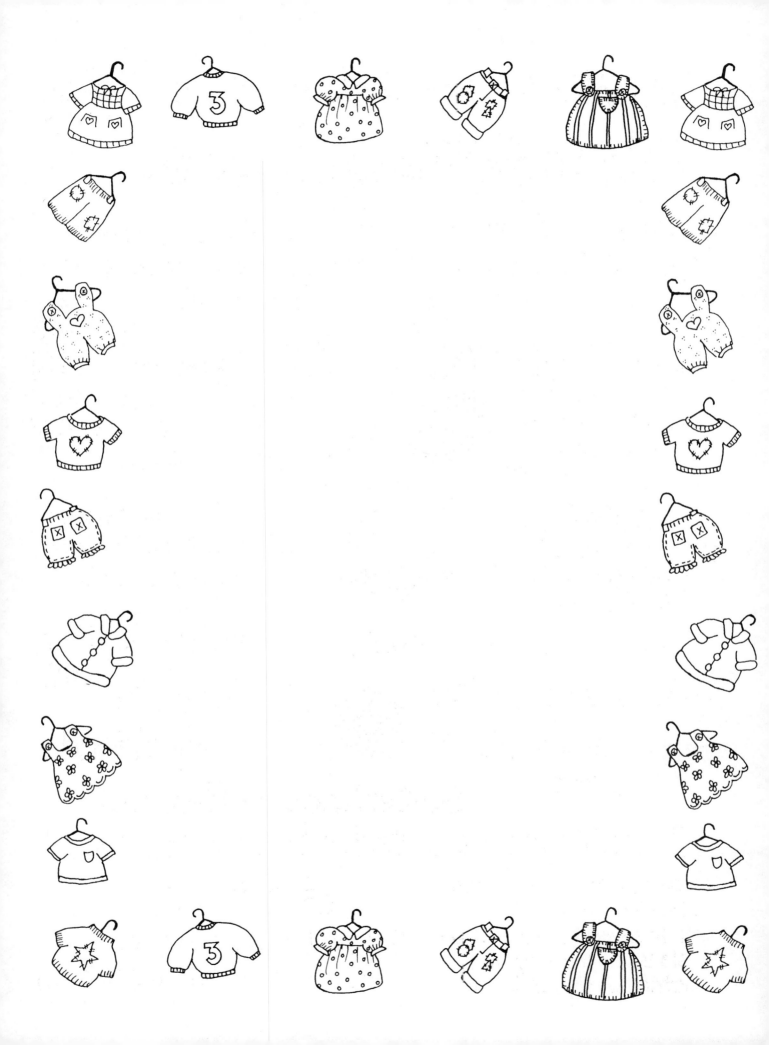

DISCOVER WILDLIFE - Have Kids

Babies Smile When Kissed by an Angel

We have a minority rule here,
It's called a baby.

In the whole wide world,
there is nothing more precious
than a baby.

Babies are bits
of stardust
blown from the
hand of God.
— Larry Barretto

SPIT
happens

Babies are such a nice way
to start people. — Herold

COUSINS
are special friends
grown from the
same FAMILY tree

Dear Sister (or Brother)
Our childhood play days may
have come to an end...
But never forget,
You are forever my friend

Here's a hug and a kiss
for the brother (sister, etc.)
I miss.

My sister,
My friend

Sisterhood is Powerful

I can't imagine a better brother than you

Oh daughter (son) so dear,
We love you more than
all the sand on the beach,
stars in the sky and
clothes on your floor!

God couldn't be everywhere,
that's why he created Godparents

31

Work is for those who don't know how to fish

Fishing

My Goal:
Fish more.
Work less.

Gone fishin'
Be back someday

Fishing
it's the reel thing

My wish:
To catch a **FAT** fish.

Well stocked rivers, lakes and streams, These are a fisherman's favourite dreams.

Captain's Quarters

WELCOME TO THE LAKE

If today were a fish, I'd throw it back.

You catch...
You clean

A fisherman's favourite line... has a worm on the end of it

Save the worms
Eat chicken

Sounds a bit fishy!

FISHING
The art of casting, trolling, jigging or spinning, while freezing, sweating, swatting and swearing. - Henry Beard & Roy Mckie

When I'm tired and I can't sleep I count fishes instead of sheep.

Haven't had much luck fishing~ but I did marry the catch of my life

An old fisherman and the catch of his life live here.

Kindred Spirits

I cherish you
You're sweet and kind,
A truer friend I'll never find

You make my Heart Smile

Our friendship is like a cup of tea
a special blend of you & me

True friends listen when no one else hears

...Friendships are glued together with kindness

To get the full value of joy you must have someone to divide it with
— Mark Twain

"Stay" is a charming word in a friend's vocabulary
— Mary Alcott

Back Door Friends Are Always Best

Share a Smile & say Hello Exchange a Kindness & watch a friendship GROW

Don't let grass grow on the path of friendship
— Native American Proverb

Friendship isn't a big thing
It's a million little things

FRIENDS like you are far and few

Life is filled with simple joys
and blessings without end
but one of my greatest joys in life
is to count you as my dear friend.

I lost my smile and you gave me yours

Friends like you
do and say
the nicest things
in the sweetest way

FRIENDS HUG THE HEART

FRIENDS
♥ Share
♥ Support
♥ Laugh
♥ Love

Friendship grows from pleasures shared.
- Charles Dickens

Special Memories
are made with
Special Friends

The only way to have a friend is to be one.
- Ralph Waldo Emerson   37

I CAN RESIST ANYTHING...
EXCEPT TEMPTATION

Entering a Positive Thinking Area

Go ahead take my advice, I'm not using it anyway.

I'm saving my husband lot$ of money
I BUY EVERYTHING I SEE...
ON $ALE!

I'm not bald
I'm just too tall
for my hair

If you're smoking in this house
you better be on fire!

If you smoke...
don't exhale

You Don't have to BRUSH all your teeth Just the ones You want to KEEP

It's been one of those days
ALL WEEK!

No BRAIN... No HEADACHE

Panic Button
Press here

A journey of 1000 steps begins with
trying to find a parking spot.

Not again.....
too much month
at the end of the money

I'm so far behind
I thought I was first

39

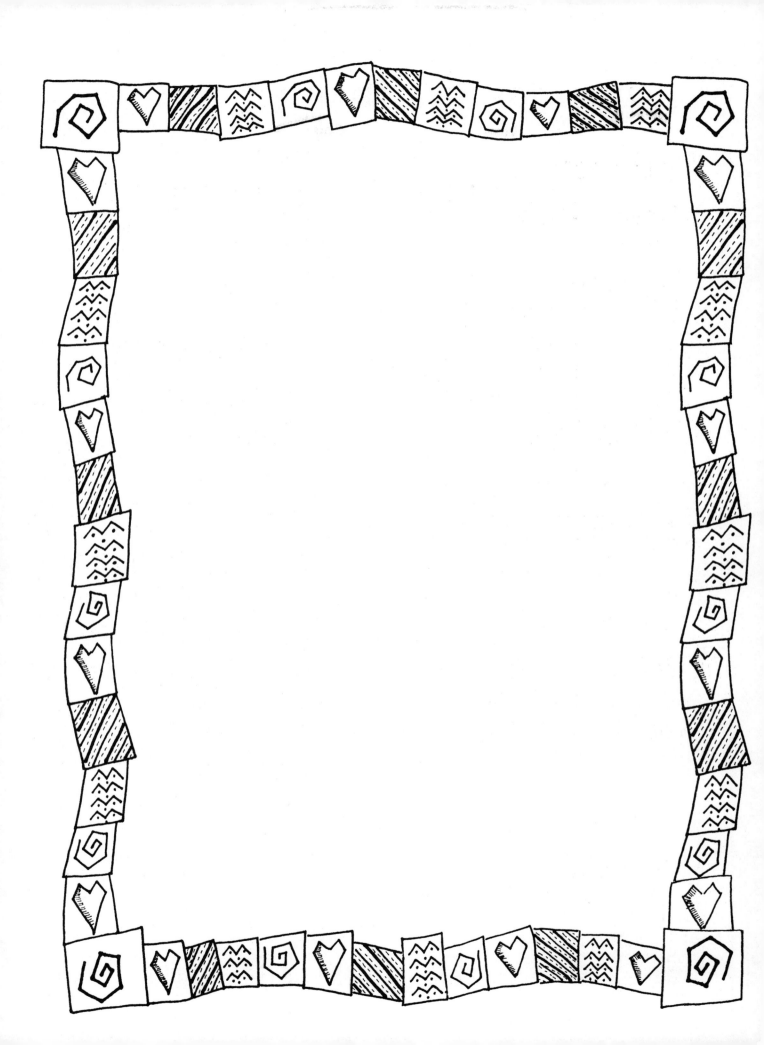

Macho doesn't prove Mucho

Real men DO ask directions.

HOME OF THE
Lawn Ranger

Men are just a bunch of animals...
but some do make good pets

Everytime I give my husband an inch
he starts to think he's a ruler!

Only Mothers of teenagers can understand
how animals can eat their young

I love to get stressed
but only when spelled backwards
(desserts)

SECRET TO DIETING
spit out anything
that tastes GOOD!

If the tv and the fridge
weren't so far apart
we'd never get any exercise

I'm not fat...
I'm just short
for my weight

**I am woman,
I am invincible...
I am tired.**

Money is the root of all evil...
and I need to feel rooted.

Girls just wanna have fund $

41

My Garden Tills My Soul

Everyone has a Mother-in-Nature

Have a Bloomin Good Day

Miracles grow where you plant them

Leave room in the Garden
for Fairies to Dance

Gardening grows the Spirit

Nurture Nature

Flower Power

A garden is a friend
you can visit anytime

I dig the earth

Nature wears a universal grin

Like life,
few gardens
have only flowers

Plant Some Kindness
Wherever You Go

43

Garden Angels are Heaven Scent

Gardening

Garden of Love Recipe
- Water with kindness
- nurture with compassion
- weed out resentment.

Earth is crammed with Heaven
Elizabeth Barrett Browning

A Sunset is Heaven's Gate Ajar

From the earth we were formed, to the earth we return.... and in between we garden

The touch of nature makes the whole world kin.
- William Shakespeare

One is nearer to God's heart in a garden, than anywhere else on earth
- Dorothy Gurney

We all need to be rooted in order to blossom

Nature is the art of God
- Dante

If you truly love nature you will find beauty everywhere
- Vincent Van Gogh

Heaven is under our feet as well as over our heads
- Henry David Thoreau

This garden is grown with love

My Best Chance For A Birdie

18

Golfer's Prayer
May I live long enough
to shoot my age

I used to WASTE my time, now I go GOLFING

To golf or not to golf?
What a silly question

I ♥ GOLF

I golf in the low 70's...
any colder I stay home

GOLFER'S 1 WISH

I'm not over the hill........ just on the back nine

SECRET TO GOOD GOLF:
HIT HARD,
STRAIGHT
AND NOT TOO OFTEN

When's Tee Time? 18

I GOLF
therefore I am not here

GOLF:
a day spent in a round
of strenuous idleness
- William Wordsworth

A person has to believe
in something
I believe I'll go golfing

Golf is a good walk spoiled.
- Mark Twain

Queen of the Green

I live with fear everyday......
but sometimes she lets me go golfing

Bye Bye Birdie

GOLF is the most fun you can have
without taking your clothes off
- Chi Chi Rodrigueez

47

Fangs for the memories and nightmares

Come in for a bite

Halloween — Boo — Boo — Boo

Mind Your Mummy & Deaddy

Sounds Fangtastic

TOMB SWEET TOMB

WELCOME EVERY-BATTY

Oops..... Bat Breath

Pumpkins come. and pumpkins go But jack-o-lanterns steal the show.

TWICK or TWEET

Love at 1st bite

TREAT...OR ELSE

The Ghostess With the Mostess!

Ghosts have real spirit!

Have A Hauntingly Happy Howl-ween

Hunters lead a WILD life

The smell of fresh sawdust
is sweeter to me,
than any rose could ever be.

Rules 4 Tools
Put 'em back or
catch the flack

Woodworkers are a cut above the board

When in doubt...
route

Sawdust means Work in Progress

Workshop Rule
Don't mess with my mess

Baseball players are rich in diamonds.

BEWARE:
Computer bytes

I craft, therefore I am.

I needle-lil love

Quiltin

Quilts are pieces
of love
Stitched together

Sew Some Sunshine

a stitch in
time
saves nine

Was there life
B 4
Bingo

BINGO

Born 2
Bingo

Dancers
have happy feet!

51

Home is Where
We hang our
Memories

Home is where we hang our memories

Bless this home with the music of laughter

Laughter is sunshine in a house

Charity begins at home
- 14th century English proverb

A small house can hold as much happiness as a large one.

Heaven seems a little closer in a house by the water

Happiness is Home Brewed

Home is where our RV is

We get along in our R.V. cuz we don't have room to disagree.

Home to laughter home to rest, home to those we love the best!

HOME is the warmth of loving Hearts

Our guests make us happy, Some in coming, Some in going

Welcome to our Zoo!

WELCOME TO OUR "wRECK" ROOM A WILDLIFE REFUGEE HABITAT

Drones Chore List
Direct From The Queen Bee's

Name	Chore	Completed

Home Swept Home!

HOUSEWORK STINKS!

No ... Martha Stewart does not live here.

Real men Do housework

House Rules

- If you open it .... close it
- If you empty it .... fill it up
- If you drop it .... pick it up
- If you spill it .... wipe it up
- If it rings .... answer it
- If it cries .... love it
- If you sleep in it .... make it up

DUST BUNNY

It's the maid's day off ... Don't trip on the dust balls

Please excuse the mess We just really want you to feel at home.

Every mother is a working mother

Cleaning your house while your kids are still growing, is like shovelling the walk before it stops snowing.
- Phyllis Diller

Around here "normal" is just a setting on the dryer

A Place for Everything And Everything in its Place
- Isabelle Beeton, 1861

Whistle While You Work
- The Seven Dwarfs

The Queen does not do dishes

An open mind opens doors

Every life is a story...
make yours a Best Seller.

Keep one secret spot
Where your dreams may go

My Life

Faith shines brightest in the dark

Problems are
Angels of
Opportunity

To discover new oceans
We must lose sight
of the shore

We can't
spell
success
without
"U."

A journey of 1000 miles begins with but a single step

- Lao Tzu

Quitters never win
Winners never quit.

Dream deep,
for dreams lie hidden in your soul
Reach high,
for every dream precedes a goal.

Do the worst first!

Don't itch for anything
that you're not willing to scratch for.

Opportunity never comes... It's here

Inch by inch
Any goal is a cinch

Carpe Diem
Seize the Day

Don't agonize - organise

No goals -
No glory

Don't be-little
Be Big.

Happiness
is just a smile away

Happiness is
an inside job

Mud thrown
is ground lost

Genius is
1 % inspiration
99 % perspiration
- Thomas Edison

Turn a frown upside down.

Laugh often,
Learn much
and love life.
With all your
Heart

Don't count the days, Make the days count.

Store recipes inside plastic
sheet protectors in a binder.

Recipe Name:

Source:

Date:

What to Put In:

How to Make It:

Special Stuff to Remember:

To create your own personal recipe book make copies of this page. Write or type your favorite recipes on each page. Add any "Special Stuff to Remember" like: " This is my Mom's apple pie recipe, which everyone LOVES! Her tip: Mix 2 or 3 types of apples together.

COVER THIS SPOT WITH A PHOTO
Example: Mom with her apple pie

Bless this Kitchen with Love & Laugter

The torch of Love is lit in the Kitchen
Polish Proverb

God Blesses This Kitchen
He doesn't clean it

THIS CHICK IS COOKIN'

I ♥ love ♥ hugs,
I ♥ love ♥ Kisses,
But don't forget,
I ♥ also ♥ love
HELP WITH THE DISHES.

Fish
to taste right
must swim
3 times...
~ in water
~ in butter
~ in wine
- French Proverb

I'd cook
if I could find the can opener

Happiness is lickin' the spoon

Spoonfuls of love added to every recipe.

Homemade with Love
from my kitchen.

Homemade and Good
4 - U - 2

61

Any Time Is Tea Time

Conserve Water.. Drink wine

Kitchen Quips

Wine is Sunlight Held Together By Water
- Galileo

I've never met a COOKIE I didn't like!

Sweety you're the of my

FLOUR CHILD

Coffee Java

From One Bag To Another: you're Tea-RRIFIC!

Life is one big tea party

To bean or not to bean?

TEA THYME

♪ Latte Da Latte Da ...

Everything you see, I owe to spaghetti
- Sophia Loren

Money can't buy love... but it can buy caffé mocchas

I only have a kitchen cuz it came with the house

Before my first cup of coffee

I'm not a bad cook if you have no taste

Peas be with you

I'm a bear!

63

Oh the Experince of this Sweet Life

- Dante

Life

View life by smiles, not by tears
and age by great moments, not by years.

Life has a way of passing you by,
passionately if you sing it,
boring if you sigh...

Another day,
Another play

I'm not sure if life is passing
me by or trying to run me over

The problem with doing nothing is ...
you never know when you are done.

If you want to
break a habit
Drop it!

One thing for sure...
there is no sure thing.

He didn't call them the 10 suggestions.

What good are laurels if you can't rest on them?

I Made a Wish And You Came True

Consider Yourself Kissed!

Love means holding hands not grudges.

Love is a hug

I love sharing life with YOU!

LIFE IS SO VERY FINE BECAUSE YOU ARE MY VALENTINE

Forget love... Let's fall in chocolate!

In the end the love you take is equal to the love you make.
— John Lennon

To love, is to receive a glimpse of heaven
— Karen Sunde

Love conquers all
— Virgil

Miles apart but always close in ♥

Love Lives Here

The happiest people in the world are the ones who help spread it!

The ♥ that loves is always young
— Greek Proverb

You make my heart flutter

Joy is a net of love
by which you can catch souls

Love can't grow
until you give some away

You take ordinary moments
and make them shine

One is very CRAZY
when in LOVE
- Sigmund Freud

Your love gives a glow to my soul

All works of love
are works of peace
- Mother Teresa

In all you dream
and all you do,
may the LOVE you share
bring sweet bliss to you

XOX
You paint
my world
with
Love

Loved you yesterday,
love you still,
always have and
always will

All you need is love
- John Lennon

You complete me
- Jerry MaGuire

You are so easy
to love

Love wasn't put in your heart to stay
Love isn't love until you give it away

69

Memories are forget-me-nots
Gathered along life's way,
Pressed close to the heart
In a perennial bouquet
-Clara Smith Reber

Memories are windows that bring the past into view
where we can glimpse again all the joys we ever knew

We Don't Remember Days
We Remember Moments
- Cesare Pavese

Memory is a Painter
It Paints Pictures of The Past
- Grandma Moses

The Heart is Like a Garden Where Sweet Memories Grow
With Life's Best Moments Tended Row by Row

Memory is the treasure
of all things
and their guardian
- Cicero

MEMORIES

Dream Weaver

The soul would have no rainbow if the eye had no tear

Keepsakes

Family memories and stories retold are like treasures as dear as gold

Who has not saved some trifling thing
more prized than jewels rare,
a faded flower, a broken ring,
a tress of golden hair
- Ellen Howarth

The Memories We Collect & Give Brighten Our Lives As Long As We Live
- Julie Sneyd

71

Grow old along with me, the best is yet to be. *Over the hill*

— Robert Browning

I shall grow old but never lose lifes zest,
because the roads last turn shall be the best.

— Henry Van Dyke

It's sad to grow old,
but nice to ripen.

— Bridgette Bardot

I'm a valuable antique
with hair full of silver
teeth full of gold
and joints full of lead

Baldness – the cure for dandruff

It's better gray than nay

Age
Is only a
Number

I'm not aging,
I just need
repotting

Look 30,
Act 20,
Feel 60
Must be 40

Cheap Facelift - SMILE

I'm not over the hill yet,
I can't get up it

Don't take life so seriously,
it's not permanent.

I've become a
Valuable, Historic Monument.

It takes a long time to grow old

— Pablo Picasso

Been there,
Done that...
Can't remember

Don't resent growing older,
many are denied the privilege

I'm too young to be this old!

Thanks For The Memories

We may not have it all together... but together we have it all

Cute as a Button

FRoM a Little Babe So VeRY SMall How & when did yoU GRow so TAll?

CK: cute kid

Presenting the Royal Highness

A PaRTy fit for a KING

Look what heaven sent

Baby's 1st Kiss MAS

It's not easy being a Princess

Life's a Beach

Girl Friends Forever

I'm a Miracle!

Fun in the Sun

a Match Made in Heaven

Fond Memories of Friends, Family & Fun times

Seasons come and Seasons go Captured here are the Sweetest Memories We Know

Hearts Forever Entwined

We is terrific!

Be humble? Impossible! We're the Grandparents!

Best Buddies

☆ Sherrif on Duty ☆

SAY CHEESE

All Stars

OOPS... CAUGHT ON MY PEST BEHAVIOR

Our Little Angels

♡ Grandma's Sweethearts ♡

A Little Peanut Batter

School Daze

☆ Grandpa's All Stars ☆

In school and up to know good

77

LIFE is the greatest bargain,
We get it for nothing — Yiddish

Do good and heaven will come down to you. — Hawaiian

A stumble may prevent a fall — Chinese

The best candle is understanding. — Welsh

You make the road by walking on it. — Nicaraguan

The more you know, The less you need — Australian Aboriginal

KIND WORDS CONQUER — Asian

The day is lost if no one has laughed. — French

The flowers of all tomorrows are in the seeds of today. — Asian

Before you marry, keep both eyes open After marriage, shut one. — Jamaican

It takes a 1000 voices to tell a single story. — Native American

New day.... New fate — Bulgarain

If you are lucky enough to be Irish, you are lucky enough. — Irish fact

79

Earth is dearer than GOLD
- Estonian

Good deeds are the best prayer.
- Serbian

Mañana is often the busiest day of the week.
- Spanish

Beauty without virtue is... a flower without perfume.
- French

God works in moments
- French

A gentle word opens an iron gate.
- Bulgarian

Hold a true friend with both your hands
Nigerian

Make haste slowly
Latin Proverb

Worry often gives a small thing a BIG shadow
- Swedish

Faith keeps the world going
- Hindi

Trust in God..... but tie up your camel
- Iranian

In dreams and in love nothing is impossible.
- Hungarian

It is better to be in chains with friends, than in a garden with strangers
- Persian

No sleep.... No dreams.
- Korean

81

Happy Bearday

Don't feed us We're stuffed.

Stuffed with Love

Best Fur-ends Fur-ever

A friend by your side Can keep you warmer than any fur coat

Friends ... make everything **bearable**

Show Me the Honey

FREE BEAR HUGS anytime... any bear

Honey Bee Happy

Bear with me

Bear Collector Orphans Welcome.

I Wish I was a teddy bear... The more worn out you are The more valuable you become.

Only the most Special Bears get their fur all loved off 83

Aa Bb Cc Dd Ee Ff

1
2
3
4
5
6
7
8
9
&
Zz
Yy

Aa Bb Cc Dd Ee

Ff Gg Hh Ii Jj Kk

Ll Mm Nn Oo Pp Qq

Rr Ss Tt Uu Vv Ww

Xx Yy Zz &

1 2 3 4 5 6

7 8 9 0

Gg
Hh
Ii
Jj
Kk
Ll
Mm
Nn
Oo
Pp
Qq

Xx Ww Vv Uu Tt Ss Rr

Practising my ABC's and 123's

A
B
C

1
2
3

A
B
C

1
2
3

A
B
C

1
2
3

A
B
C

1
2
3

Practising my ABC's and 123's

ABCDEFGHIJKLMN
OPQRSTUVWXYZ

ABCDEFGHIJ
KLMNOPQRS
TUVWXYZ

ABCDEFGHIJ
KLMNOPQR
STUVWXYZ

med dk gold
+ = med dk teal blue
| = backstitch:
    med dk gold

Four Longer Poems

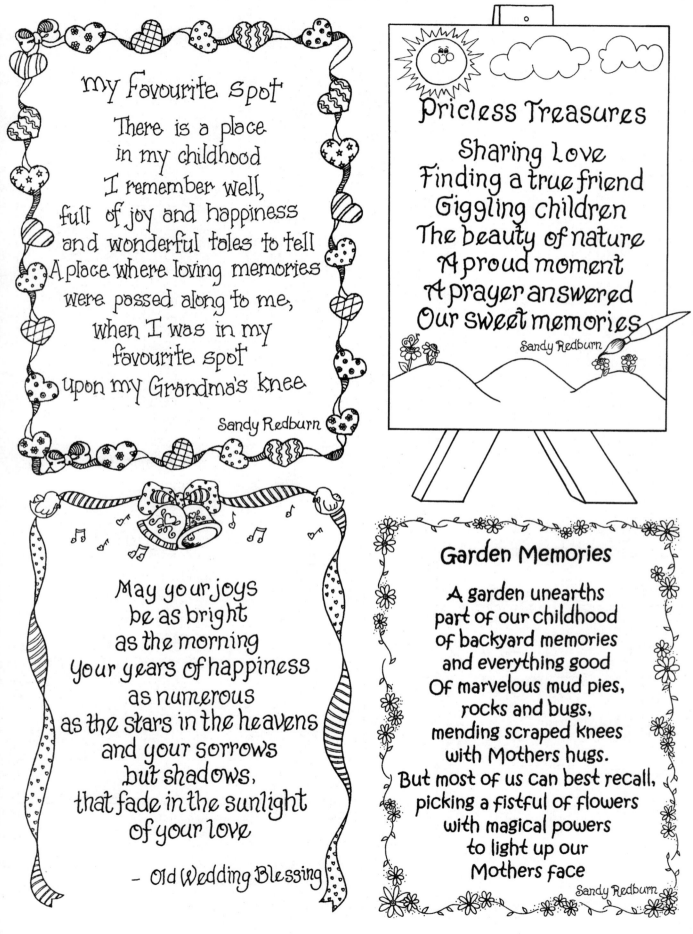

My Favourite Spot

There is a place
in my childhood
I remember well,
full of joy and happiness
and wonderful tales to tell
A place where loving memories
were passed along to me,
when I was in my
favourite spot
upon my Grandma's knee

Sandy Redburn

Priceless Treasures

Sharing Love
Finding a true friend
Giggling children
The beauty of nature
A proud moment
A prayer answered
Our sweet memories

Sandy Redburn

May your joys
be as bright
as the morning
Your years of happiness
as numerous
as the stars in the heavens
and your sorrows
but shadows,
that fade in the sunlight
of your love

- Old Wedding Blessing

Garden Memories

A garden unearths
part of our childhood
of backyard memories
and everything good
Of marvelous mud pies,
rocks and bugs,
mending scraped knees
with Mothers hugs.
But most of us can best recall,
picking a fistful of flowers
with magical powers
to light up our
Mothers face

Sandy Redburn